Our Wo...

C000142284

Written by Monica Hughes

Collins

The world can be hot,
cold, dry and wet.

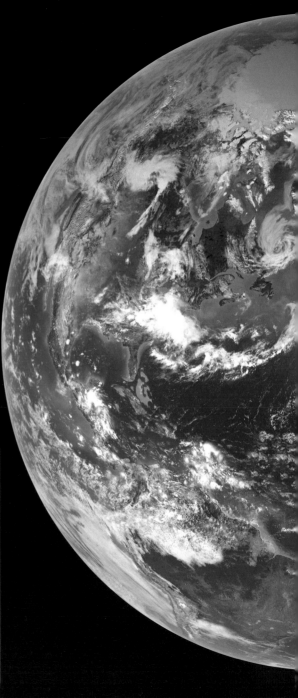

2

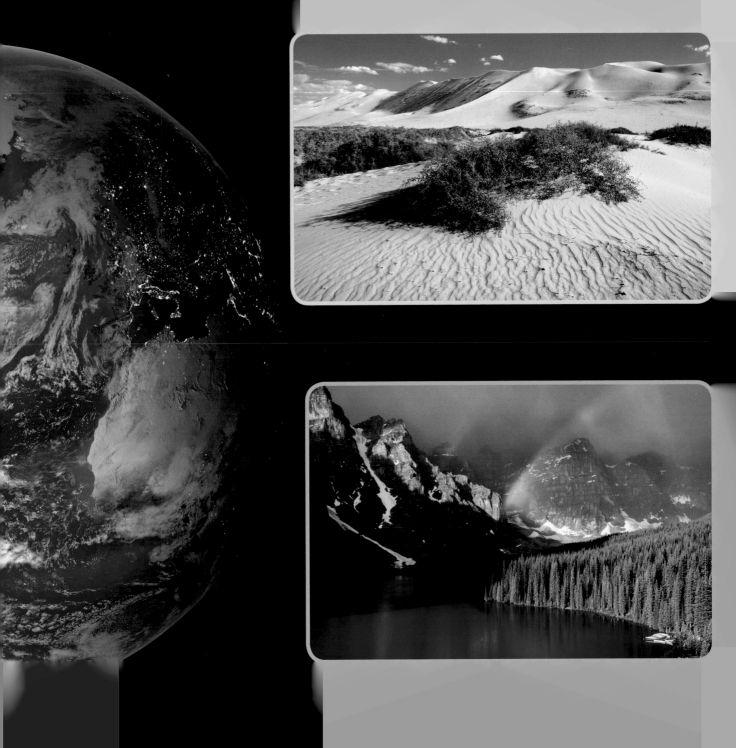

It is cold and icy at
the North and South Poles.

North and South Poles

It is cold and wet in the mountains.

6

mountains of the world

It is hot and dry in the deserts.

deserts of the world

It is hot and wet in the jungles.

Some places are sometimes hot, sometimes cold, sometimes wet and sometimes dry!

Our world

14

15

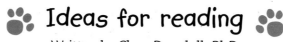# Ideas for reading

Written by Clare Dowdall, PhD
Lecturer and Primary Literacy Consultant

Learning objectives: children read and understand simple sentences; they demonstrate understanding when talking with others about what they have read; children know about similarities and differences in relation to places

Curriculum links: Understanding of the world: The world

High frequency words: about, the, some

Interest words: world, different, weather, icy, North and South Poles, places

Resources: internet, weather recording chart, whiteboard, globe or atlas, materials for creating a landscape, place names on cards, sticky notes

Word count: 73

Getting started

- Look at a globe or an atlas. Help children to understand that the poles are the coldest places, and the equator is the hottest place.

- Look at the front cover. Ask children to describe what they can see, e.g. *cold, misty mountains.*

- Read the blurb on the back cover and discuss the different types of weather in the world, making a note of them on the whiteboard.

Reading and responding

- Ask children to read pp2–3 aloud. Check that children recognise that the central image is the world from above.

- Reread the text on p2. Look at how commas are used to separate the list of describing words. Ask children to describe each inset photo and match it with the relevant describing words from the list: *hot, cold, dry, wet.*